Piano Etudes
Book 4

for the development
of musical fingers

Selected and Edited by Frances Clark, Louise Goss and Sam Holland

Study notes by Phyllis Alpert Lehrer

Copyright © 1990 Summy-Birchard Music
a division of Summy-Birchard Inc.
All Rights Reserved   Printed in USA
ISBN 0-913277-27-4

Contents

Preface

For generations, collections of etudes have been readily available to piano teachers and their students. Why should we create yet another? The answer lies in the impracticality of many existing collections and in the genuine scarcity of well-selected materials for elementary and intermediate levels. The great teacher-composers of the nineteenth century who wrote such splendid etudes were creating technical studies for advanced pianists. Those written for elementary and intermediate students were seldom carefully graded and often unbalanced in technical content.

This series attempts to fill that gap. In our own teaching we find a great need for the experiences these etudes provide. In making the choices for these four volumes, our objectives were to:

1. choose the best and most useful etudes, ones that are musically as interesting as possible without crossing the line into repertoire with multiple technical issues.
2. provide a balance of experiences for both hands, for all ten fingers and in all keyboard topographies.
3. grade the etudes into collections that provide a logical, balanced and natural development of the technical skills required in repertoire at the corresponding level.

In these collections, good pedagogy is a higher priority than total authenticity to primary sources. Transpositions have been suggested in Books I and II to provide more complete experience in the topography of different keys. Revisions have been made where one difficult spot overshadowed the main value of an etude or better to meet the goals outlined above. In a few instances, no piece could be found for an important subject and so we created it ourselves. In such cases, no composer is listed.

In teaching these etudes, remember that the genuine value of an etude, like any exercise, begins after the student has worked it out carefully and can play it securely. It is through many repetitions, always judged and guided by the ear and by the ease and comfort of the physical sensations, that the student will increase tempo and facility and improve in tonal beauty and control.

The invaluable practice suggestions by our colleague, Phyllis Alpert Lehrer, are designed to focus the student's attention on:

1) the musical shape and direction of each phrase
2) how to project these most easily through physical sensation, choreography and breathing.

We believe these etudes and the practice suggestions will benefit you and your students as much as they have benefitted us and ours.

Frances Clark, Louise Goss and Sam Holland

3

1. Five-Finger Patterns and Scales

Trills combined with scales

Wolf

4

Czerny

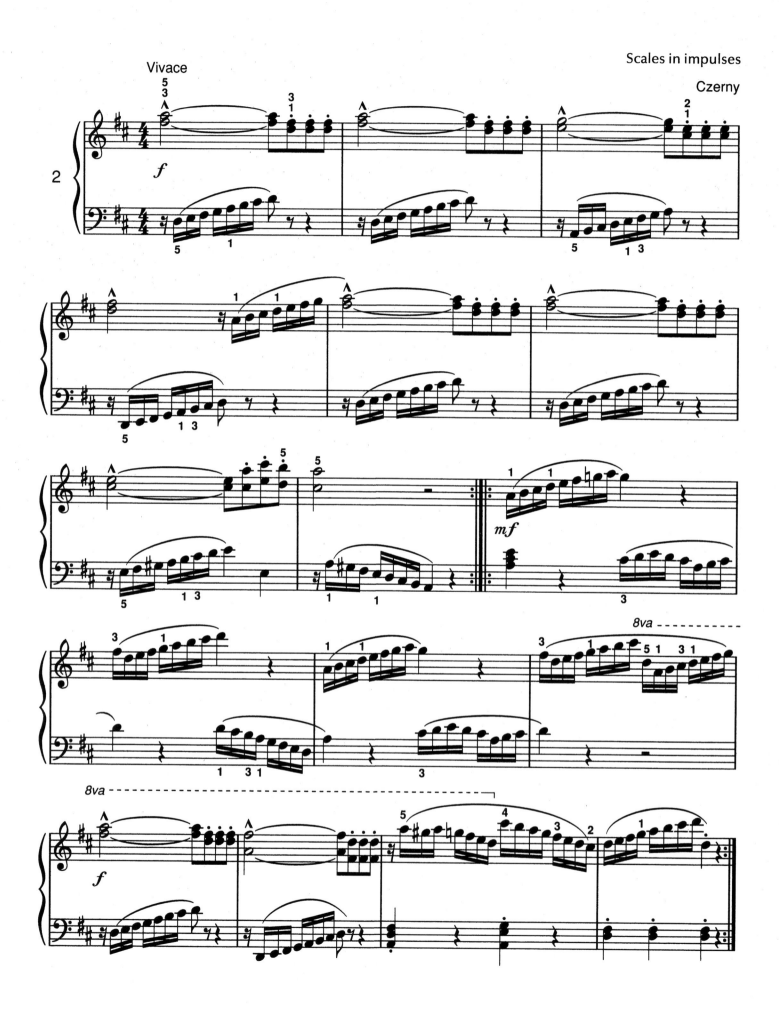

5

Ascending and descending left-hand scales

Köhler

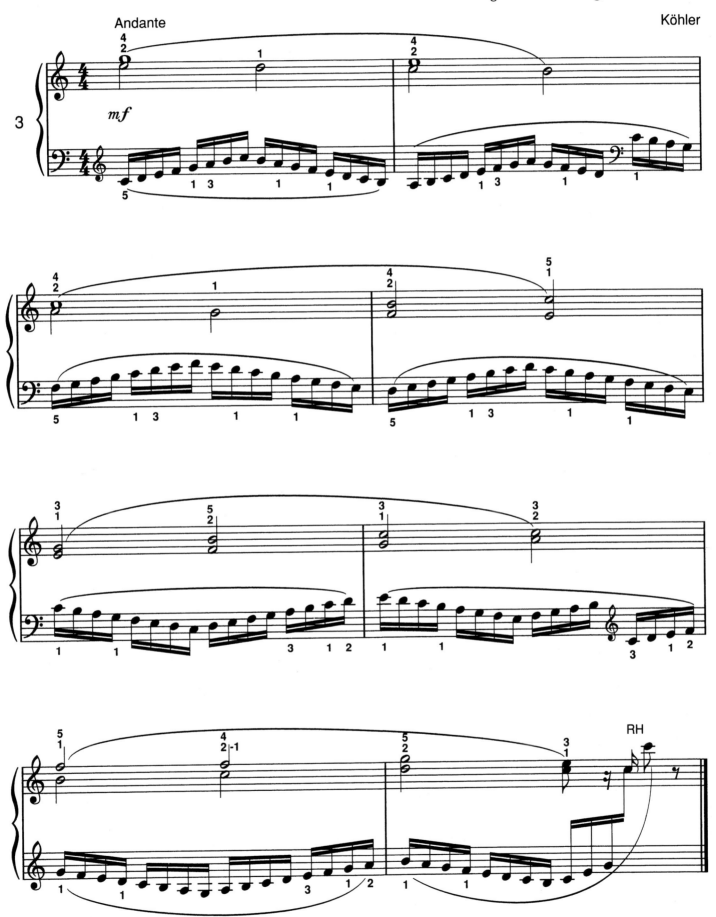

6

Lengthening scale impulses for right hand

Czerny

Right-hand scales with left-hand accompaniment
in sustained and moving voices

8

Right-hand chromatic scales

Czerny

Allegro vivace

6

cresc.

8va

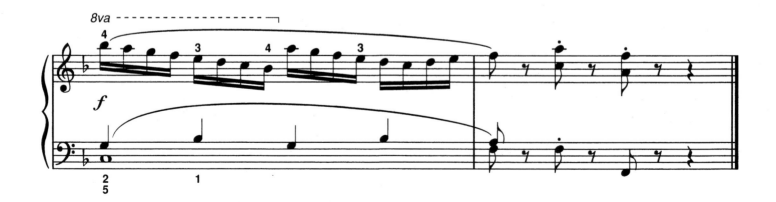

Czerny

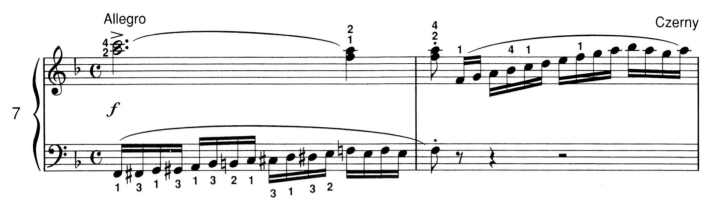

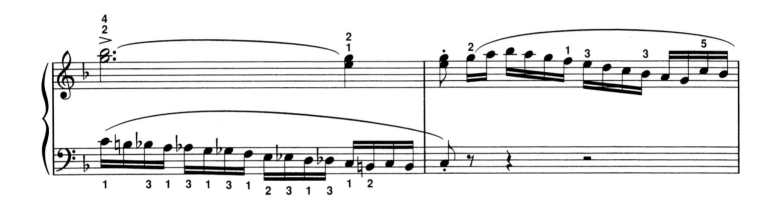

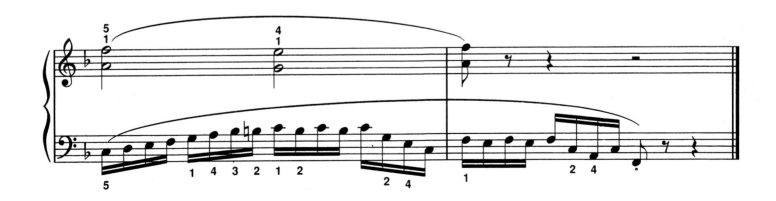

10

Left-hand scales combined with
arpeggiated right-hand figures

Heller

2.   Arpeggios

Arpeggiated broken chords combined with scales

Czerny

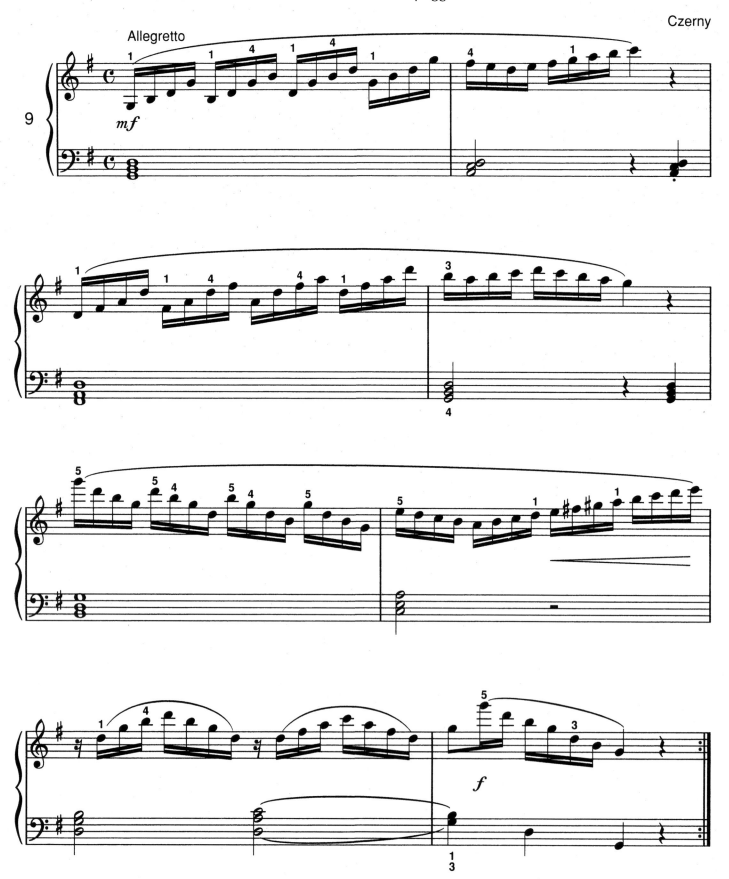

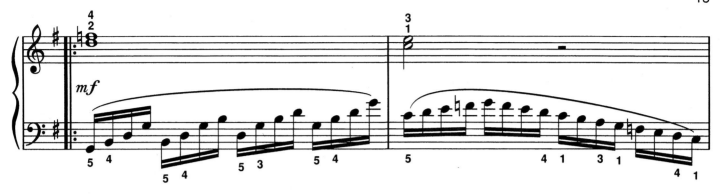

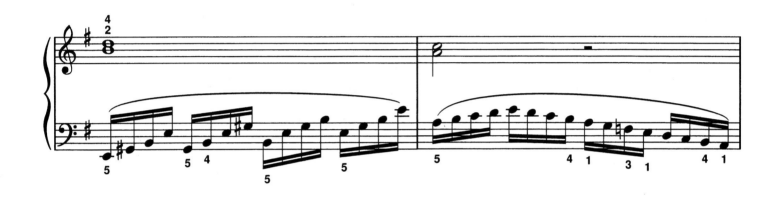

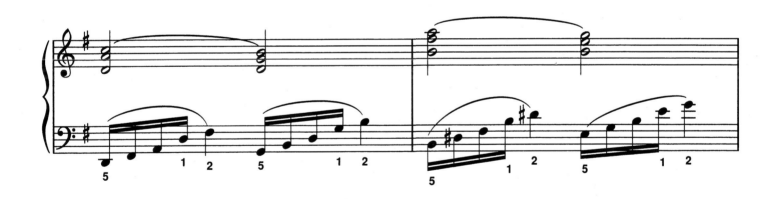

14

Czerny

10

Two-octave arpeggios, ascending and descending

Czerny

3. Chords and Broken Chords

Three- and four-note chords with quick position shifts

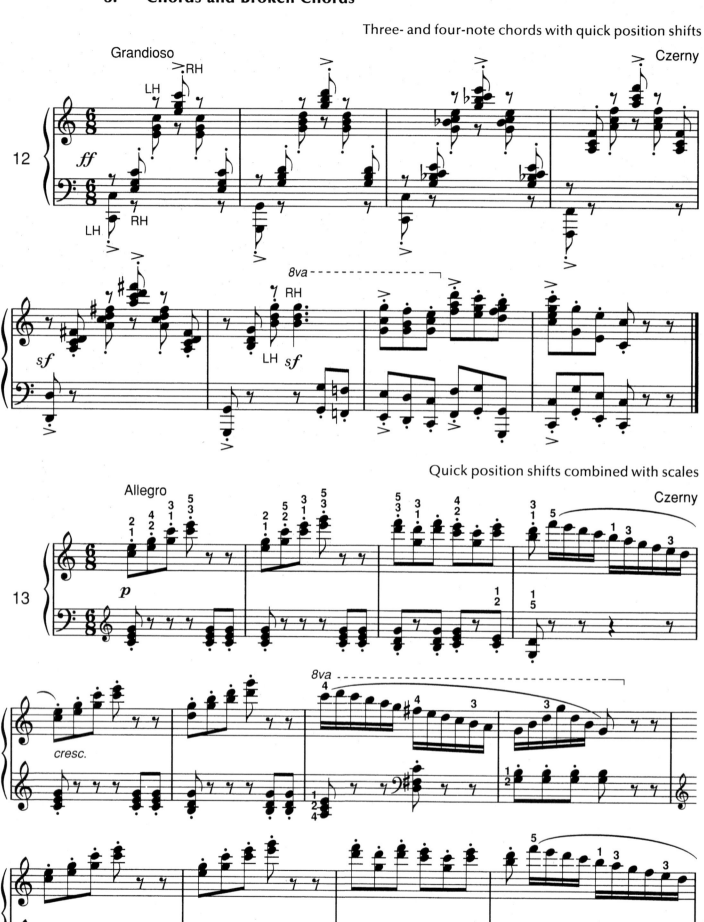

Quick position shifts combined with scales

4. Thirds, Sixths and Octaves

Legato thirds combined with chord leaps

Czerny

Rapid consecutive sixths

Giocoso

Lebert

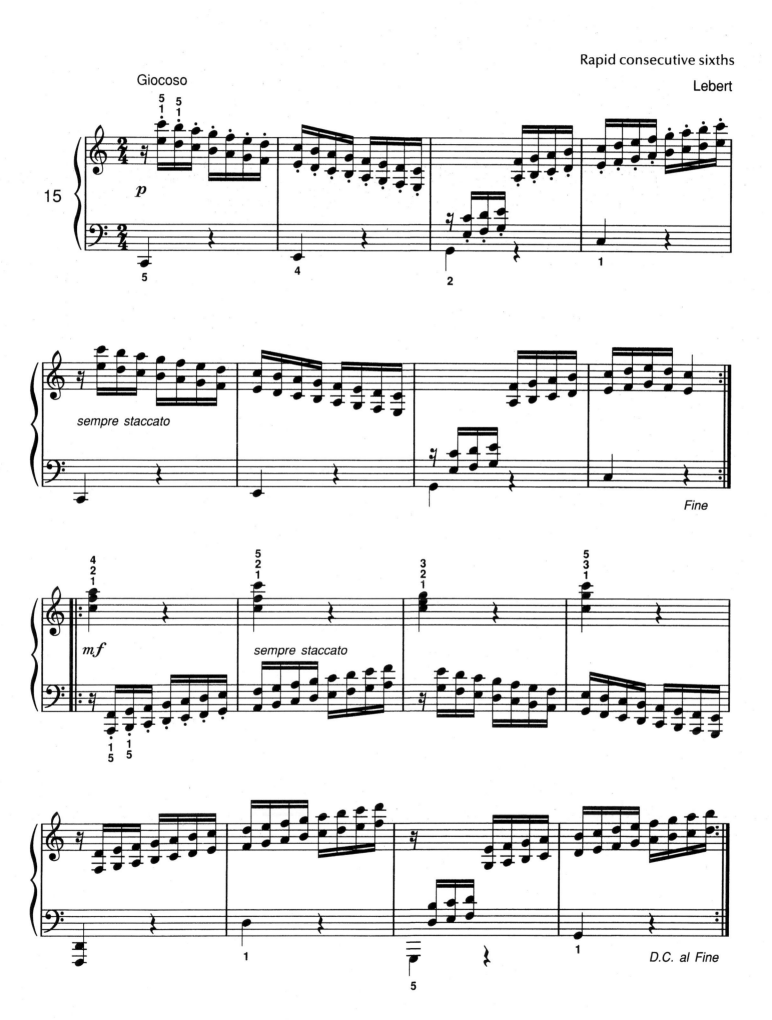

Octave extensions with position shifts

Lemoine

Consecutive octaves

Bertini

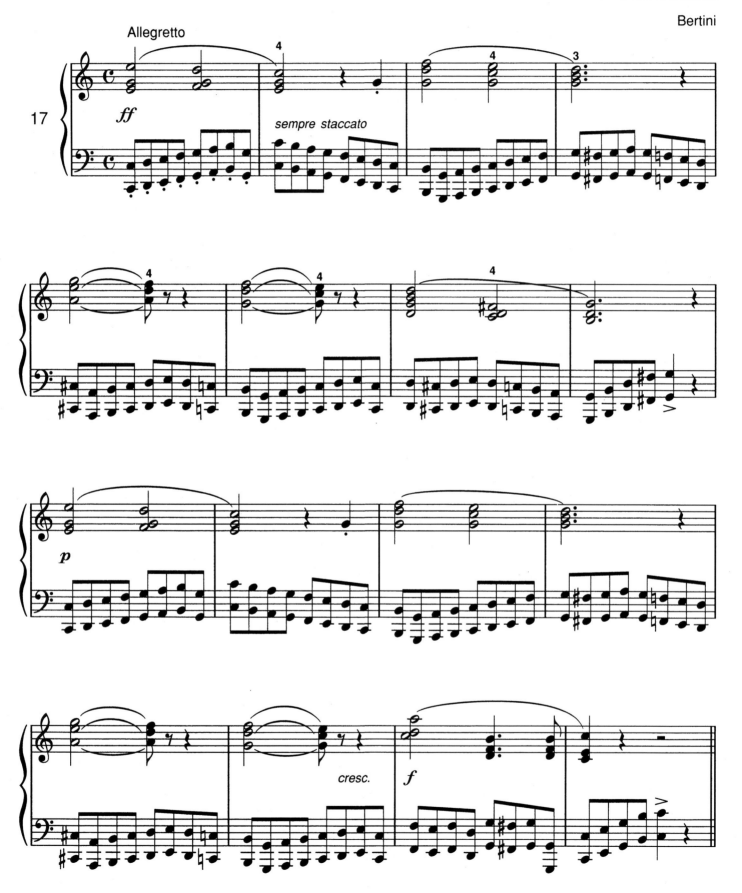

24

5.   Melody and Accompaniment

Right-hand melody with
Alberti accompaniment

Czerny

Rapid accompaniment with outside of left hand
doubling the melody in tenths and other intervals

Czerny

Rapid figures with melody implied
by the outside of the hand

Czerny

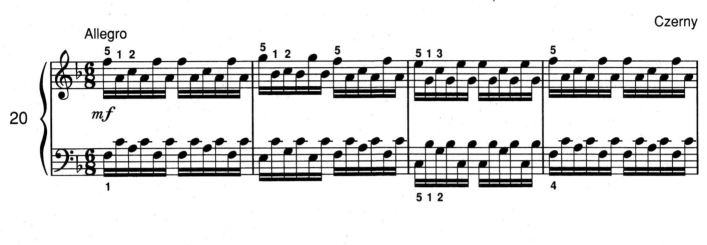

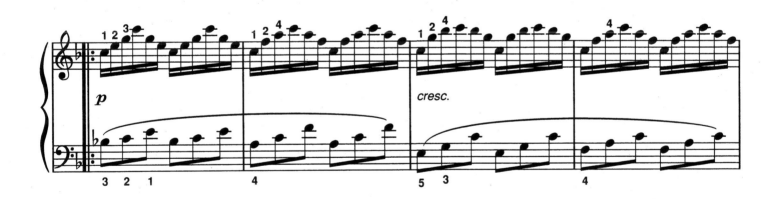

6.   Special Subjects

Rapid repeated notes in right hand

Czerny

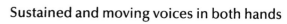

Sustained and moving voices in both hands

Czerny

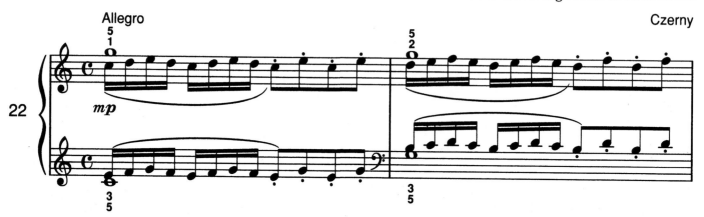

28

Melody crossing hands with broken-chord accompaniment

Streabogg

Fine

D.S. al Fine

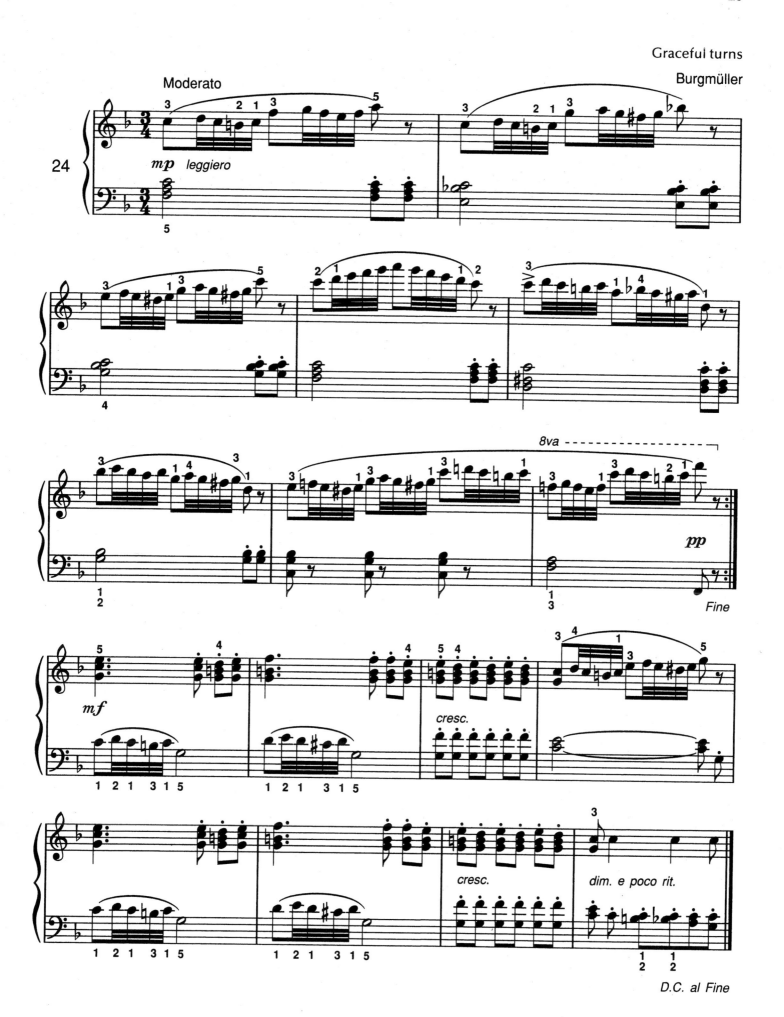

Graceful turns

Burgmüller

24

Alternating hands with leaps up to a twelfth

Lemoine

Practice Suggestions

1. Observe the four-bar phrase structure and the melodic outline formed by the first note in each group of sixteenth notes.

Use forearm rotation for even, fluid trills. Use a rolling motion of wrist and arm for notes that connect the trills.

Play the scales, articulating with your fingertips and using circular arm motions. In general, crescendo as you ascend, decrescendo as you descend. Use small rotations to make the scale crossings easier.

2. In each measure of the A section, use a down-up motion in both arms. In left-hand scales, use inward or outward circular motions, and small rotations for the crossings as you ascend.

In the B section, use a down motion in both arms on the first and third beats of each measure. Rotation is helpful where there is a sudden change of direction (example measure 15) as well as in ascending left-hand crossings.

3. In this etude, feel the left-hand scales in down-up impulses of one measure, connected by circular arm motions. Be sure your arm moves to support your fingers, moving inward when ascending and outward when descending.

Use a lighter arm for beats 3 and 4 of each measure. The exception is the last measure where you need to swing the right arm in a vigorous semi-circle for the final octave, C to C.

4. Play through this etude slowly, treating all accompaniment patterns as blocked chords. Use down-up motions with both arms, corresponding to the rhythmic inflections of the phrases. Hear how the two-measure units build an eight-measure phrase structure.

Play the scales articulating with your fingertips and using circular arm motions. Use rotation to facilitate scale crossings and in sudden changes of direction.

In playing the Alberti accompaniment, use forearm rotation to increase ease and flow. Fingertips always feel the key surface, with no lifting.

5. Play through this etude slowly, right-hand melody as written, blocking the left-hand chords. Increase arm weight to bring out the harmonic tension in measures 3 and 7, lighten the arm as the tension resolves in measures 4 and 8.

Play the right-hand scale patterns with circular motions outward from the body. Use forearm rotation in the scale crossings, trill figures (measures 2 and 4) and the broken chords (measures 7 and 8).

Play the left-hand with small circular motions, "down-up-up," ending on the tip of a weightless thumb. Hold the dotted quarter notes with a light fifth finger.

6. In the right-hand chromatic scales of this etude, use rotary motion when fingerings alternate (1-3, 1-3, etc.) and circular motions when fingering is consecutive (4-3-2-1, etc.). Lean into the phrase goals on half notes, releasing your weight with an upward motion of wrist and arm on the third beat of measures 2, 4, 6.

Let the left hand support the melody with slow rotations between quarter notes. Drop lightly into the fifth finger and then release weight, holding it as lightly as possible.

7. In this companion etude for left-hand chromatic scales, use rotary motion when fingerings alternate and circular motions when fingering is consecutive. Also use rotary motion for the trills at the end of measures 1 and 3 and the beginning of measure 8.

Use fluid down-up motions of the arm to organize each measure except in measures 7-8 where two down-ups per measure help to clarify the rhythmic shape.

8. This etude combines arpeggiated figures with scales. Use rotary motion toward the inside of the hand to help articulate the arpeggiated figures. Play the scales with down-up impulses, circular motions and small rotations at the crossings.

In the chordal sections, drop arm weight directly into firm fingers. Then soften the hand immediately, rising buoyantly out of each chord. This creates resonance rather than harshness. Use a faster key descent into the *forte* accented chords, a slower descent with "grasping" fingertips for the *piano* staccato chords.

9. The sweep of this virtuosic etude requires a long line felt in eight-measure phrases.

Play the right-hand ascending arpeggiated figures with firm fingertips, and an open hand. Move your arm to support each finger as it plays, circle in, then out of each 4-note figure, moving away from the body as you ascend. Begin the descending figures with your upper arm away from your body, circling from out to in.

Play the left-hand ascending arpeggiated figures in the same way, but circling out, then in.

Because scales cover less distance across the keyboard, reduce the size of your circular motions in scale passages.

In measures 13–14, practice the left-hand arpeggiated figures, first blocked, then as written using circular motions outward from the fifth finger and inward toward the second finger. Drop into the next similar figure.

10. The waltz-like character of this etude can best be expressed with a down-up-up motion in both arms. As your arm lightens, use more finger tip.

Before playing the etude as written, practice the accompaniment figures separately. Feel the left-hand accompaniment as "drop-lighter-lightest."

In playing the arpeggiated figure of the melody, move the arm freely away from the body with a circular motion, being sure the elbow feels buoyant. Use rotation at each arpeggio crossing.

11. To achieve the *energico* quality of this etude, feel the swirl from lowest to highest notes. Use circular motions for ascending and descending arpeggios.

In the right hand, feel the fleshy left corner of the thumb as you begin the arpeggio. Support your fifth finger with a free arm as you begin to circle back toward the inside of the hand.

In the left hand, feel the fleshy tip of your fifth finger as you begin the arpeggio. Support your thumb with a free arm as you begin to circle back toward the outside of your hand.

Use rotation to increase facility in measures 13, 14, 15.

12. To feel the big pulses of this etude, drop arm weight into beats 1 and 4, letting these chords ring slightly longer than those on other beats.

Be sure the fingertips are firm, but soften your hand immediately as the tone is produced.

Allow your whole body to move with the arms from the lowest to highest part of the keyboard. In the last two measures, drop your weight in front of you, thinking, "in-in-in" and putting the greatest emphasis on beats 1 and 4.

13. This etude combines quick position shifts with scales. Use a feeling of down-up-up to establish the lilt of the $\frac{6}{8}$ meter. Use circular arm motions to direct the shape of the musical lines. Keep the top notes bright.

Play the accompaniment so that it supports the musical direction—$\frac{6}{8}$ down ♪♪♪ up-up-down, etc. Experiment with voicing left-hand chords to the lowest note and to the highest note—which line do you want to hear?

14. Begin practice of this etude by playing the first and last chords of each measure, omitting the sixteenth notes. After the down beat, lighten the arm as you move through the rests to the upbeat.

Practice the legato thirds hands separately, with a tiny bounce on each note to help create balance and evenness of tone. As you increase the tempo, begin the first two sixteenths with an up motion of the wrist and arm, arriving at the third sixteenth with a downward motion.

15. In this etude, shake the sixths out from the upper arm into firm fingertips with buoyant, elastic wrists. Begin each two-measure phrase by taking a breath on the sixteenth rest. Drop lightly on the downbeat in measures 2, 3, 6, 8, etc.

Your arm should always support your fifth finger. Be sure to play on the corner of the thumb.

16. In this etude, play the octave extensions with a fluid hand, wrist, elbow and upper arm. Be sure to play on the tip of the thumb.

Make a small outward circle to the first octave and a larger one into the half note.

The accompaniment should be felt as down ♪♪ up-up-up/down. Drop into the downbeat and play the eighth-note upbeats as light-lighter-lightest.

17. In this etude, drop the arm weight lightly into each octave, letting the upper arm and elbow choreograph the melodic line with inward and outward circular motions. In the B section, use a more lateral arm motion for the smaller distance of the phrases.

Coordinate the motion between arms with a buoyant feeling between the strong beats 1 and 3.

18. In this etude, play the bouncing staccato melody with firm fingertips and a light arm, the two-note slurs with tiny circular motions. In the last measure, combine circular motion with rotation.

In the Alberti accompaniment, use rotation, keeping the fingertips on the keys with no lifting.

19. Before playing this etude, practice the right-hand melody with the bottom notes of the accompaniment, omitting the repeated sixteenth notes. This helps establish the lilt of the $\frac{6}{8}$ meter and the shape of the musical line.

When playing the melody as written, use small circular arm motions as you move from one measure to the next, creating four measure phrases.

When playing the accompaniment as written, use rotation to achieve facility and flow. Keep the fingertips on the keys with no lifting, rotating to send weight into the outer fingers. Feel the left hand open for the finger change from beats 3 to 4; in measure 4, open the hand for the octave, and contract as you move from 2-1 to 3-1 to 4.

20. Before playing this etude, practice lines 1, 2 and 4 by outlining the melody and accompaniment notes on beats 1, 3, 4, 6, omitting the inner voices.

Then practice these lines slowly as written, using rotary motions with the most energy to the fifth finger on strong beats.

In line 3, circular motions replace rotation. Begin this line with a lighter arm and more finger articulation to bring out the new melodic shape and texture.

21. Before playing this etude as written, outline the melody by playing a single note for each beat. Then combine this single-note melody with the left-hand as written, feeling your wrists and arms circle from down to up as they move from beats 1 to 2 and 3 to 4.

When playing the melody as written, feel each fingertip taking over the same spot on the key for the repeated notes as the wrists and arm rise slightly. In measures 5 and 7 the right hand must use more lateral motion for the repeated figures. In measures 6 and 8, choreograph the melodic shape with circular and rotary motions.

22. Before playing the four voices of this etude, practice the moving inner voices (hands separately and hands together) without the whole notes. Use small semi-circular motions for the sixteenth notes and down-ups for the staccato eighths.

Next practice hands separately, feeling an internal "play-release" on the whole notes, allowing the inside of the hand to remain fluid for the moving voices.

23. Before playing this etude, block each measure to experience the harmonic progression which shapes each phrase. In the B section select the melodic tones that clarify the harmony.

Then practice the right hand separately. In the A section, use outward circular motions to travel out of the half notes across the keyboard. In the B section, combine circular motions with rotation.

In playing hands together, coordinate the hands by feeling a down-up from beats 1 to 2 and 3 to 4. Throughout the piece the rhythmic emphasis is strongest on beat 3.

24. Before playing this etude, practice the melody and accompaniment, omitting the turns.

Then practice hands separately. Choreograph the melody with the turns as "down-roll-up, down-roll-up." To achieve graceful turns, articulate with your fingertips and use a light, rolling arm.

Be sure the accompaniment moves the phrases across the barline. Play the eighth notes with a light arm. Use an upward motion of wrist and arm on beat 3 to lead naturally to a drop into the next downbeat.

25. When playing this etude, use up-down motions to project the upbeat character of the motives. In large leaps, increase the upward circular motion and the involvement of the upper arm, feeling "airborne."

The staccato notes must be played with finger articulation and a light arm. The hand that leads each phrase should play with slightly more tone than the hand that follows.